ONTARIO

JOURNEY ACROSS CANADA

Harry Beckett

The Rourke Book Co., Inc.
Vero Beach, Florida 32964

Harry Beckett M.A. (Cambridge), M.Ed. (Toronto), Dip.Ed. (Hull, England) has taught at the elementary and high school levels in England, Canada, France, and Germany. He has also travelled widely for a tour operator and a major book company.

Edited by Laura Edlund
Laura Edlund received her B.A. in English literature from the University of Toronto and studied Writing for Multimedia and Book Editing and Design at Centennial College. She has been an editor since 1986 and a traveller always.

ACKNOWLEDGMENTS
For photographs: Geovisuals (Kitchener, Ontario), The Canadian Tourism Commission and its photographers.
For reference: *The Canadian Encyclopedia, Encarta 1997, The Canadian Global Almanac, Symbols of Canada. Canadian Heritage*, Reproduced with the permission of the Minister of Public Works and Government Services Canada, 1997.
For maps: Promo-Grafx of Collingwood, Ont., Canada.

Library of Congress Cataloging-in-Publication Data

Beckett, Harry. 1936 -
   Ontario / by Harry Beckett.
     p. cm. — (Journey across Canada)
   Includes index.
   Summary: An introduction to the geography, history, economy, major cities, and interesting sites of Canada's second largest province.
   ISBN 1-55916-198-1 (alk. paper)
   1. Ontario—Juvenile literature. [1. Ontario.]
I. Title II. Series: Beckett, Harry, 1936 -   Journey across Canada.
F1057.4.B43   1997
971.3—dc21
                                    97–2214
                                    CIP
                                    AC

Printed in the USA

TABLE OF CONTENTS

Hudson Bay

HUDSON

BAY

LOWLAND

James Bay

CANADIAN

SHIELD

● Hemlo

Lake
Superior

Sault Ste. Marie
Sudbury ●

Georgian
Bay

Ottawa ●

Kingston ●

Lake
Huron

**GREAT LAKES
PLAIN**

Toronto

Lake Ontario

Hamilton ●
● Niagara Falls

Lake Erie

N

W   E

S

PROVINCE OF ONTARIO

Chapter One

SIZE AND LOCATION

To drive across Ontario from east to west takes about 24 hours. Ontario is Canada's second largest province, nearly twice the size of Spain.

Look for its shape in Central Canada. In the north, it stretches to the icy shores of Hudson Bay. To the east and west lie Québec and Manitoba. In the south, Ontario is on the same **parallel** (PER uh lel) as northern California. There it shares four of the Great Lakes with American states.

About 8 million of its over 10 million people live in cities. Many of these cities are on the waterways that first carried trade across rough land. Later, railways were built and small towns grew along them. Some northern settlements can still be reached only by small plane.

Find out more...

- Ontario's total area is 1 068 580 square kilometres (412 611 square miles).
- The Great Lakes are Superior, Huron, Erie, Ontario, and Michigan. All but the last border Ontario.

Chapter Two

GEOGRAPHY: LAND AND WATER

Ontario has about 25 000 lakes, mostly in the two, huge northern regions—the Hudson Bay Lowland and the **Canadian** (kuh NAY dee un) **Shield** (SHEELD). Many lakes were scooped out by the glaciers that once covered a large part of North America.

Most of northern Ontario is in the Canadian Shield, an area of rock, forests, and lakes.

Settlers in Ontario occupied farmland that was divided into rectangles

The land around Hudson Bay and James Bay is a region of **muskeg** (MUS keg) and **permafrost** (PUR muh frost), where trees can hardly grow and few people live.

The Canadian Shield covers about two-thirds of the province. It is heavily forested, very rocky, and rich in minerals.

Gentler, greener land with **fertile** (FUR tile) soil forms the Great Lakes Plain. Most of Ontario's 10 million people live here.

Chapter Three
WHAT IS THE WEATHER LIKE?

Southwestern Ontario has some of Canada's warmest summers and mildest, shortest winters.

As you move north, the winters become colder and longer until, 1600 kilometres (994 miles) away, on Hudson Bay, winter stays until spring is turning into summer in Niagara Falls. In the snow belt, which gets westerly winds from the Great Lakes, snow falls mostly between the months of December and March.

Average temperatures are warmer in the south and cooler in the north, but bodies of water have an effect also. Lakes never heat or cool as much as the land nearby. Winds blowing off lakes cool the nearby land in summer and warm it in winter.

Find out more...

- The hottest temperature recorded in Ontario was 42.2°C (108° F) in Biscotasing.
- The coldest temperature recorded in Ontario was -58.3°C (-72° F) in Iroquois Falls.

Over 400 000 people annually come to ski at Blue Mountain in Collingwood on Georgian Bay

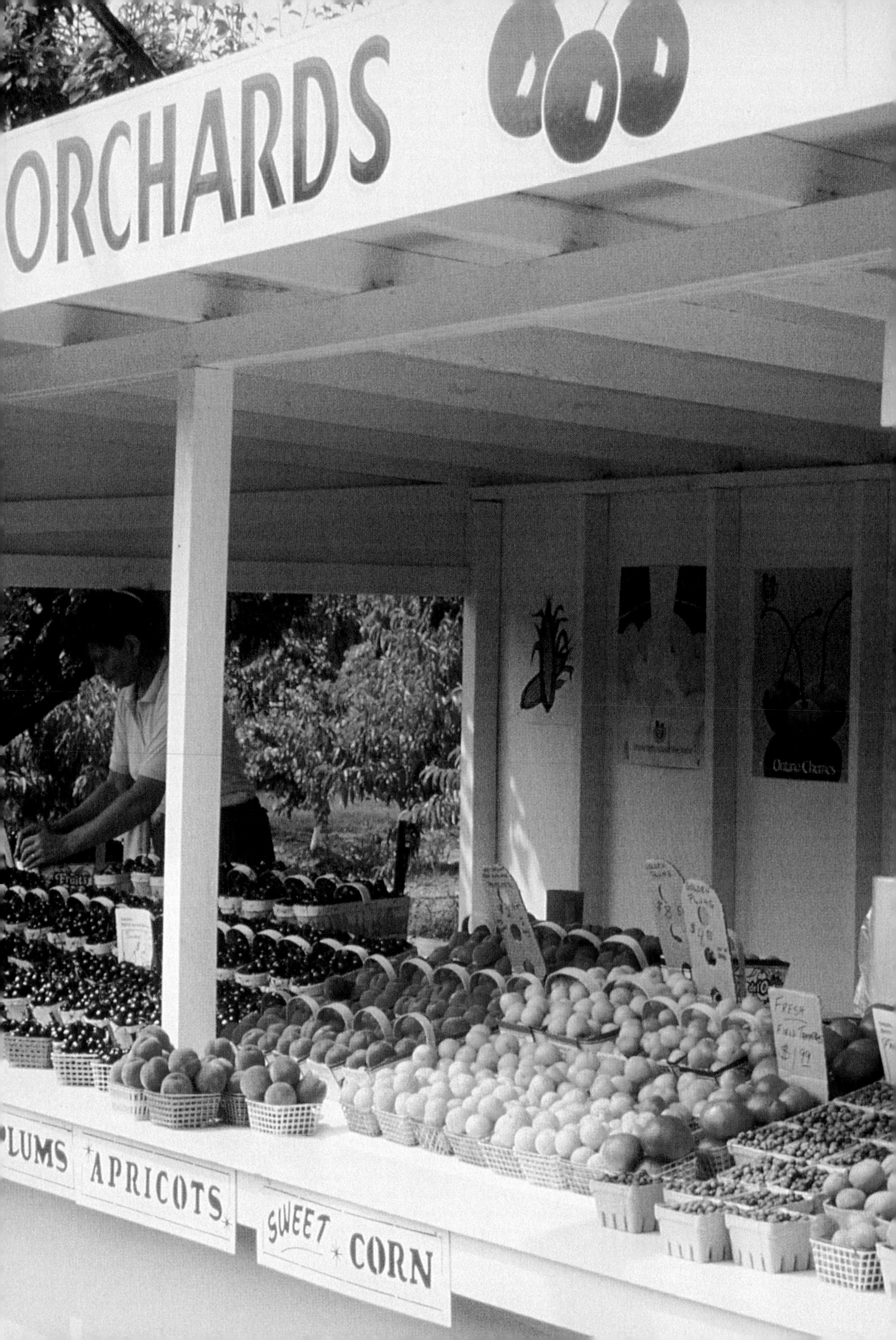
ORCHARDS
PLUMS
APRICOTS
SWEET CORN
FRESH

Chapter Four

MAKING A LIVING: HARVESTING THE LAND

Once, forests covered most of Ontario. In the south, early settlers cleared much of it for farmland and timber.

Now the farms of this fertile land and mild climate produce livestock, corn, vegetables, and fruit. However, housing and industrial development are taking away the precious farmland in areas such as the Niagara Peninsula.

The forests of the Canadian Shield are cut to make wood and paper products. The trees cut down are replaced by seedlings, but some people worry that too much logging and mining will spoil the landscape and the wildlife **habitat** (HA bih tat).

In the north hunting, trapping, and fishing are an important part of the economy.

The Niagara area is noted for its many fruit farms

Find out more...

- Ontario fruit includes grapes, apples, peaches, pears, and berries.
- The Niagara Peninsula is the land between Lakes Ontario and Erie.

Chapter Five

FROM THE EARLIEST PEOPLES

When the Europeans arrived in the seventeenth century, there were two main groups of Native peoples living in Ontario. The Native peoples of the Canadian Shield fished, hunted, and trapped. Those who lived farther south farmed.

The Europeans traded furs and got involved in local conflicts. Many Native peoples died in the conflicts and from diseases the Europeans brought.

The historical site of Ste. Marie Among the Hurons, with a moat around the fort which gave protection and access by canoe

At Fort Henry in Kingston on Lake Ontario, British redcoats fire a salvo.

The French and their Native allies controlled the region until the British defeated them in 1763. During the American Revolution (1775-83), the British used the area as a base. Some Americans loyal to Britain moved across the border.

Early immigrants came mostly from Europe for land and opportunity, but in recent years people have arrived from all corners of the world and changed the face of Ontario.

Chapter Six

MAKING A LIVING: FROM INDUSTRY

People call Ontario the Heartland of Canada. Many valuable minerals are mined in the Canadian Shield. Cities like Hamilton and Sault Ste. Marie use iron to make steel. Much of it goes to the busy automobile industry. This and other high-tech industries are becoming very important.

Many of Ontario's rivers help to produce the power these industries need. The province also uses **nuclear power** (NOO klee ur POW ur) to make electricity.

Three quarters of the province's wealth comes from what are called service industries— transportation, public administration, and trade in goods, money, and information.

Find out more...

- Sudbury, in the north, produces about one fifth of the world's nickel.
- Sir Adam Beck Power Station on the Niagara River opened in 1903.

A gold mine in Hemlo, in the Canadian Shield

Chapter Seven

IF YOU GO THERE...

If you go to Ontario, don't miss Toronto and its CN Tower, the world's highest free-standing structure. At its foot lies the SkyDome, home to baseball's Blue Jays.

People from all over the world visit Niagara Falls. On its way from Lake Erie to Lake Ontario, the Niagara River drops with a roar over the Canadian, or Horseshoe, Falls and the American Falls.

Throughout Ontario there are lots of places to explore and have fun at—such as Ste. Marie Among the Hurons, Ontario Place, the Ontario Science Centre, and Science North.

The red and gold leaves of fall, winter snow, and year-round lakes, rivers, and forests offer sport and relaxation.

Raincoated and rubber-booted, tourists in a cave under the Falls

Find out more...

- The CN Tower is 553 metres (1814 feet) high.
- The SkyDome's roof can be opened or closed in twenty minutes.
- The Horseshoe Falls are 55 metres (180 feet) high.

Chapter Eight

MAJOR CITIES

About nine of every ten people live in the cities and towns of the Great Lakes Plain.

Once called York, Toronto is the capital of the province, and its biggest city. It lies on the shore of Lake Ontario. Historically the surrounding land was good for farming and the nearby rivers carried trade.

Toronto seen from Lake Ontario, with the SkyDome and CN Tower

Ottawa, the Parliament Buildings, and Ottawa River

Toronto is now a city of many cultures, business, and industry. It has road, rail, and water routes and a large international airport.

Ottawa was a small community called Bytown when Queen Victoria chose it as the capital of Canada in 1857. The Rideau Canal, which runs through it, freezes in winter to become one of the world's longest skating rinks. Ottawa residents are proud of their national galleries and museums.

Chapter Nine

SIGNS AND SYMBOLS

Ontario's flag is the Red Ensign with the Union Jack of Britain in the top quarter. The province has always had close ties with Britain. Ontario's coat of arms is in the flag's centre.

The coat of arms has the cross of St. George, the patron saint of England, above three maple leaves from the Canadian forest. Green and gold are Ontario's official colours. The moose on the left, the deer on the right, and the bear on the top represent its rich wildlife.

Ontario's history is summed up by its Latin motto, which means "Loyal it began, loyal it remains."

The provincial flower is the white trillium.

Ontario's flag, coat of arms, and flower

GLOSSARY

Canadian Shield (kuh NAY dee un SHEELD) —
a horseshoe-shaped area of rock covering
about half of Canada

fertile (FUR tile) — rich, good for growing
things in

habitat (HA bih tat) — where people, animals, or
plants live; their natural environment

muskeg (MUS keg) — a swampy area of moss
and other growth that cannot carry much weight

nuclear power (NOO klee ur POW ur) — using
atomic energy to produce electricity

parallel (PER uh lel) — a line on the map joining
points at the same distance from the equator

permafrost (PUR muh frost) — ground that is
always frozen, either at, or just below the surface

*The frozen Rideau Canal, with the Peace Tower and Parliament
Buildings on the skyline*

INDEX